FURNITURE
OF CLASSICAL GREECE

BY T. H. ROBSJOHN-GIBBINGS

Furniture of Classical Greece   *(1963)*
(WITH CARLTON W. PULLIN)

Homes of the Brave   *(1954)*
(WITH DRAWINGS BY MARY PETTY)

Mona Lisa's Mustache   *(1947)*

Good = bye, Mr. Chippendale   *(1944)*
(WITH DRAWINGS BY MARY PETTY)

THESE ARE BORZOI BOOKS
PUBLISHED BY *Alfred A. Knopf* IN NEW YORK

Frontispiece Stool, folding stool, and table in the court-
yard of the House of the Dolphins, *circa* 110 B.C., on the
island of Delos. Photograph by Loomis Dean for *Life*.
© 1961 Time Inc.

FURNITURE OF CLASSICAL GREECE

BY T. H. ROBSJOHN-GIBBINGS *AND*
CARLTON W. PULLIN

 ALFRED A. KNOPF: NEW YORK

L. C. catalog card number: 63–17054

THIS IS A BORZOI BOOK,

PUBLISHED BY ALFRED A. KNOPF, INC.

ACKNOWLEDGMENTS

We wish to acknowledge our indebtedness to the scholars and the museums of the world for the information they have given us on the ancient furniture of Greece, and particularly to Gisela M. A. Richter, whose book *Ancient Furniture, a History of Greek, Etruscan and Roman Furniture* is the outstanding source of knowledge in this field. We also wish to thank the following people for their help and support: Mr. John Papadimitriou, General Director of Archaeology in Greece; Mr. John Milliadis, Curator, Acropolis Museum, Athens; Mr. Dietrich von Bothmer, Curator of Greek and Roman Art, Metropolitan Museum of Art, New York; Mr. Brian F. Cook, Metropolitan Museum of Art, New York; Mrs. Mary Carolou; Mrs. Athina Rossolimos; Mrs. Nicholas Goulandris; Mrs. Anna Douzenis; and Mr. Yerassimos Podimatas.

We are deeply grateful to Their Majesties King Paul and Queen Frederica of the Hellenes for opening the exhibition of this furniture in Athens

Fourth century B.C. bronze statue of Athena, patron deity of craftsmen in Greece.

We dedicate this book to Susan and Eleftherios Saridis and to the designers and craftsmen of ancient Greece and their living descendants

CONTENTS

FURNITURE
OF CLASSICAL GREECE

Greek bronze support of a candelabrum showing a girl seated on a klismos. This model of a chair inspired our research on the Greek furniture shown in this book. Photograph copyright the British Museum, London.

FOREWORD

This is the story of the re-creation and exhibition of the Greek furniture illustrated in this book.

In 1933, after four years in the United States, I was designing interiors for a London firm. I missed New York. I was bored. Fashionable English rooms were an indigestible mixture of Queen Anne, Georgian, and Spanish styles. The international atmosphere was foreboding. There was subconscious unrest and subconscious fear.

On Saturday afternoons I often went to the British Museum. And there, while wandering around Roman Britain and ancient Greece, I happened to see a bronze miniature chair on the base of a Greek candelabrum. As I discovered later, it was a Greek chair called a klismos. Looking at the painted Greek vases with new eyes, I saw chairs, couches, stools, chests, and tables.

It is difficult to describe my excitement. I was familiar with all of the standard types and the fashionable periods of furniture. But they did not inspire me as a designer. I was beginning to see that time, status requirements, pomp, and power had laid a heavy hand on furniture. Some of it was beautiful. Most of it, sagging with centuries of elaboration, was old and lifeless.

On Greek vases I saw furniture that was young, untouched by time. Klismos chairs curved with the delicate grace of a new moon. Folding stools poised on deer legs. Lion claws of bronze supported tables. Vitality, surging through the human figures on the vases, surged through this furniture. I had wandered unsuspecting into a new world.

Every weekend I hurried to the British Museum. Every evening in my flat I drew Greek furniture in perspective, studying variations and details. Soon it became as familiar to me as all other furniture. I could tell at once the design of

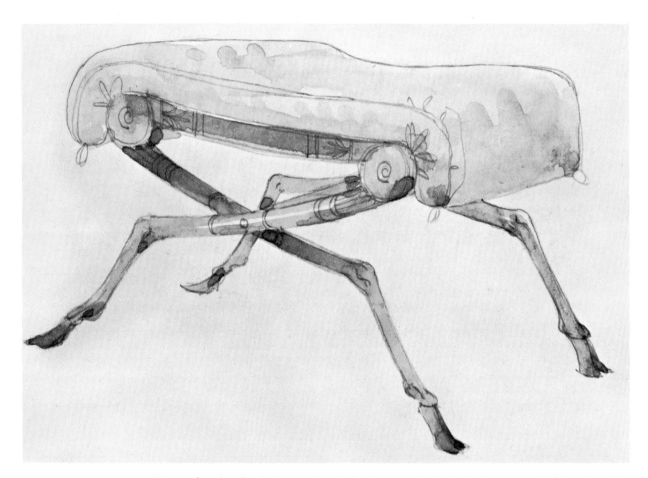

Watercolor sketch of classical Greek furniture made by T. H. Robsjohn-Gibbings in 1934.

a half-hidden stool or chair. I knew the design of fabrics shown with the furniture. I knew how the furniture was used and the Greek life surrounding it.

In Europe on holiday, I studied thousands of Greek vases. Eventually I had over two hundred drawings of Greek furniture.

In 1936, my drawings with me, I returned to America, and rented an office at 515 Madison Avenue in New York. I intended to design contemporary furniture and interiors based on Greek models. First I had to see Greek furniture in reality.

14

I gave a young cabinetmaker, Harold Bartos, drawings for six models which he was to make. Now I needed a Greek interior for the furniture.

Thirty-five miles south of Thessaloniki, the classical Greek city of Olynthus had been excavated by archaeologists from Johns Hopkins University. In a villa, which the expedition named "The Villa of Good Fortune," was a typical classical Greek room. The floor had a plain border, wide enough for couches, surrounding a mosaic panel made of multicolored pebbles. In the center of the mosaic, Dionysus, god of wine, rode a chariot drawn by panthers preceded by a horned satyr and attended by a winged Eros, surrounded by satyrs, fauns, and dancing maenads. I decided to duplicate the room in my studio.

With the help of Professor David M. Robinson, director of excavations at Olynthus, photographic enlargements of the original pebble mosaic were made and marble chips that duplicated each pebble were glued to the photograph. Completed, marble chips and photograph were laid in wet, pale orange cement. Weeks later, the cement hardened, the top surface was ground away. I watched. The Italian workmen watched. No one was sure what would happen. Then, as if they were apparitions under the sloshing film of dust and water, we saw the lunging panthers and the flowing garments of Dionysus. We shouted, laughed, and squatted down to wipe the muck away with our hands.

When the Greek furniture arrived the room was ready. Unpainted white plaster walls had been rubbed with white wax. Double doors finished in bronze and a copy of a bronze brazier found hidden under a floor at Olynthus were all in place. We carried in the chairs and tables, the Tanagra figurines and the marble bowls filled with flowering quince. Together with my staff I drank a toast to Greece and the future. That night when everyone had gone I sat and looked around the room. I had no sense that the chairs and tables in front of me had been designed over two thousand years ago. Time was powerless, nonexistent.

That was in 1937. In the following years, the press described my furniture as classical. Sometimes in houses in California, Texas, and New York, I used accurate re-creations of Greek models. More often, instead of using the actual forms,

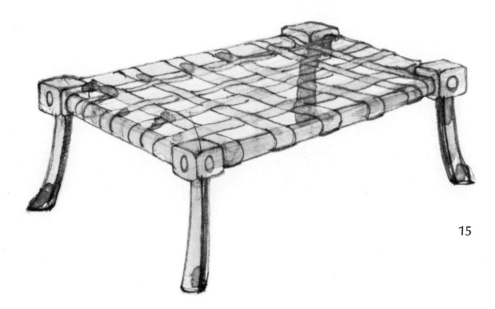

15

Watercolor sketch of classical Greek furniture made by T. H. Robsjohn-Gibbings.

I tried to recapture the spirit that made them timeless. When World War II came, I closed my studio, abandoned my mosaic floor. An era had gone.

Americans seize instantly on a new fashion. Postwar American householders seized on "modernity." Houses became "machines for living," furniture an "organic" adjunct, synthetic fibers "miracle" fabrics. Buildings that housed corporations became "corporate images."

In 1946, ignoring the fashionable plastic, plywood, and metal approach to furniture, I attempted to bring timeless design to Grand Rapids. Ten years later, leaving greedy assembly lines and hungry home furnishing floors to their own devices, I returned to my private clientele and custom-made furniture.

In 1960, during our annual visit to Greece, Carlton Pullin suggested we

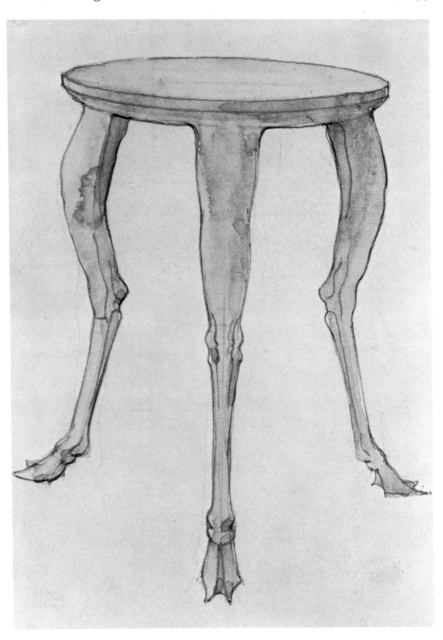

16

review my early research and have the authentic Greek designs made in Greece. We met Susan and Eleftherios Saridis, who are deeply interested in Greek archaeology and are the owners of one of the finest cabinetmaking plants in Europe, Saridis of Athens. Later that year, when they came to the United States to study production methods and visit relatives—Susan was born here of Greek parents—we decided that together we would make and exhibit a collection of Greek furniture in Athens in the spring of 1961.

My original notes and drawings were carefully re-examined, new discoveries in Greece and elsewhere were checked, and while Carlton did further research, I re-created the models for the exhibition. In the swamp lands of the Po delta in Italy, the Etruscan city of Spina had recently been uncovered, and in the Greco-Etruscan burial areas, hundreds of pieces of various forms of Greek pottery were found. Many of these were decorated with drawings of Greek furniture unknown to the modern world. On one, a red-figured kylix, or drinking cup, discovered in 1957, Carlton found the design of the couch, or klini, shown on pages 114, 115. We went to Rome, Paris, and London to examine new additions of Greek pottery in museum collections, and added our findings to our research file.

Finally, nineteen designs were selected for the exhibition, all dating from the sixth to fourth centuries B.C. (Since the exhibition, three models have been added to the collection.) Full-size detail drawings and models made in New York were sent by air mail to Saridis of Athens. A plaster model of the bronze leg shown on page 100 was flown to New York from Palermo, cast in bronze, and flown to Athens. Photographic enlargements of Greek vases, the sources of most of the furniture designs, were also sent to Athens. Finally, a date was set for the exhibition. It would open on May 31, 1961, and would be attended by Their Majesties King Paul and Queen Frederica of the Hellenes.

Press releases were mailed to American and European magazines and newspapers. *Life* magazine, taking up our suggestion that the furniture be photographed in ancient Greek sites, decided to send photographer Loomis Dean to Athens. It was April. There was nothing more to do in New York. We flew to Rome for a rest, and seven days later we arrived in Athens.

Everything was ready. Everything was waiting. Skillful Greek hands were applying the final coat of wax to the models. We looked. What was there to say? Eleftherios had executed every design superbly. That night at dinner with Susan and Eleftherios we poured a libation of retsina wine to Athena, goddess of craftsmen.

But we were soon stunned to learn that it is strictly forbidden to transport and photograph objects on the ancient, historical sites in Greece. No one had told us. Loomis Dean would arrive any day. We pleaded. Heads shook. It was impossible. Or was it? Behind the scenes gentle persuasion was at work. One week later,

Susan ran into the exhibition room waving a piece of paper. It was the final permission.

Paradise for *Life* photographers would be holocausts seen through a lens. So I thought looking at Loomis Dean, handsome, well-tailored, armed with glittering photographic equipment. His contempt for all things unphotogenic was devastating. My heart sank. If only we could photograph the furniture in an earthquake or a volcano. If only we could blow up the Parthenon again.

I called a taxi. It is a ten-minute drive from the Grande Bretagne Hotel to the Saridis showroom, where the exhibition was installed. We drove past the colossal temple of Olympian Zeus. It looked minute. Trader Horn was going to a tea party. Carlton, Susan, and Eleftherios were waiting. We went upstairs to the exhibition.

Early next morning we were at the Keramikos, the ancient cemetery of Athens, with Mr. John Milliadis, the wise and patient curator of the Acropolis Museum. On one of the high mounds is a copy of the famous grave monument, the stele of Hegeso, shown on page 63. The original is now in the National Archaeological Museum in Athens. One of our models, a klismos, was re-created from this stele. We were to photograph our chair alongside the carved model. We carried the chair from the van and placed it in the grass and poppies at the base of the stele. The morning sunlight was brilliant. The chair carved in marble and the chair in walnut were identical. The angle of the sun was perfect. I heard Loomis Dean shout, "Stand back." I saw him leap to the opposite mound. Nobody moved. There was an arrogant click. *Life* had made its first kill.

The days went racing by. I remember hundreds of American sailors crowding around us as we carried the furniture in-between the soaring columns of the Temple of Zeus, near the Acropolis. I can see Loomis prowling around the white marble temple of Poseidon at Sounion, watching the blue shadows, crouching down to find a camera angle, and waving back a crowd of Scandinavian tourists.

Mr. John Papadimitriou, General Director of Archaeology in Greece, led us through Vraona, the newly excavated maze of colorless earth and stone, once the fifth century B.C. Sanctuary of Artemis. In awe we watched the spades of the excavators probe the black mud. Mr. Papadimitriou reached down. In his hand was a tiny clenched fist of white marble. Spellbound we converged toward it.

Our friend Cecelia Ager, a writer and critic on her first visit to Greece, was with us. Like a child listening to a fairy tale she followed Mr. Papadimitriou as he led us to the foundations of the stoa. Fragments of walls enclosed a group of rooms with stone floors and tables made of blocks of stone supporting marble slabs. In the floors, between the tables and walls, were holes, and in some were bronze fragments of the legs of couches or beds that had been inserted there.

Here was irrefutable evidence of the dimensions of a classical Greek couch. I looked at Carlton. We had the couch from the exhibition in the van. How

18

would its dimensions compare with the couches of Vraona? I whispered to Susan. She hurried over to the van. I heard Carlton tell Cecelia to watch and pray. The couch was carried across the caking mud. Gently, slowly it was lowered into place, where its prototype had been over two thousand years ago. Susan said something in Greek to Mr. Papadimitriou. I heard Cecelia shout, "It fits." I looked at Carlton. The legs of our couch were exactly over the holes in the stone.

It was imperative that we go to the island of Delos, to the famous Greek villas of the second century B.C. The furniture had been photographed against public monuments and temples. I wanted it shown against the domestic background of ancient Greece.

The mosaic floor of the andron (men's quarters) in the Villa of Good Fortune at Olynthus, Greece, excavated by Professor David Robinson for Johns Hopkins University. From *Excavations at Olynthus, Part VIII* (The Johns Hopkins Press).

Susan rented a boat, the *Iris*. We met at dawn on the docks of Piraeus. The furniture was already on board. We rowed out, climbed aboard, met the captain and the two crewmen, and prepared ourselves for what might come. We would spend the night on the island of Kea and be in Delos the following day. Now a party of six, including Cecelia, Jane Lester, a staff member of Radio Free Europe, Susan, Loomis, Carlton, and myself, we waved to the lighthouse keepers, skirted around a mammoth aircraft carrier, and moved out into the Aegean Sea. It looked enormous.

Exhausted, I settled down on a mattress on the raised cabin deck, my back against a tarpaulin covering the furniture. I could hear Loomis, Jane, and Cecelia tearing the hierarchy of magazines and newspapers limb from limb. With a blanket over my body, my head under a pillow to protect me from death by sunstroke, I said the hell with it and slept. So did Susan and Carlton.

The best part of sailing is walking across a gangplank onto dry land. That evening at the island of Kea we not only walked on firm ground, we walked from the gangplank into a restaurant directly opposite. The Saridises' chauffeur, Taki, and the captain hauled out what Cecelia called a fine, honorable table. Carlton mixed drinks from the generous supply placed on board by Eleftherios, and Susan vanished into what she called, with Greek optimism, the kitchen. We ate, gossiped, argued, watched the stars come out, and later jammed ourselves into our miniscule cabins and slave-quarter berths. In the morning we sailed to Delos.

Island of the sun, birthplace of Apollo, Delos today has no inhabitants except the guards. No sound came from the island. Silently we glided toward a shoreline of white shattered marble piled up between decapitated columns. Through my binoculars, I could see the ruined villas half way up a low hill. At the end of the small stone jetty two guards were waiting. Susan produced our official papers. A mild argument began. Nearby, a man was beating an octopus against a rock, and at his feet a large turtle tied by one flapper to a wooden stump was lunging in circles in the shallow water.

After the furniture was uncovered and unloaded, Susan and the guards started along the jetty, and the men carrying the furniture followed. Turning to Loomis and Jane, I shouted, "Forward to victory!" Cecelia and Carlton at the end of the jetty waved to us to hurry. The sun was already high.

The path, a narrow line of orange dust, wound between gray rocks coated with olive green lichen. Like a *millefleurs* tapestry, fields of wild flowers were laced with bright scarlet poppies as far as the eye could see. The cool wind blowing across the island had the faint aromatic perfume of thyme.

Below us the ruined town was a jumble of whiteness framed by a gray-green coastline and an unearthly blue sea. Susan called out a direction and waited with Taki behind a crumbling wall. The guards were unlocking an iron gate between two massive pylons. We had arrived at The House of the Dolphins.

20

(Opposite Page) The re-created Greek room in the New York office of T. H. Robsjohn-Gibbings in 1937 showing a part of the mosaic floor copied from the pebble mosaic floor found at Olynthus, Greece.

Intruders from another world, we walked across the white mosaic floor of an entrance hall into a peristyle court. White monolithic columns, with delicate flutes carved on the upper half, stood proudly like sentinels around a recessed floor of mosaic. In the four corners, cupids held onto leaping dolphins with harnesses of gold, and in the center, wide borders of wave and meander designs made a sweeping circle.

We brought in the furniture. Loomis looked like a hawk about to grab a sleeping lamb. I was fearful. I suspected that under the mosaic floor was a deep well for storing water. The guards warned Susan that only one person at a time in his stockings could walk on the mosaic. We lifted down the furniture and gingerly pushed it into place. Cecelia and Carlton gathered poppies for a vase we had brought along. We waited in the cool shadow of the wall. Loomis the artist went into action.

It was time to move on. The procession re-formed, we stopped for pictures against the crumbling theater, then went down narrow streets lined with poppies to the tourist restaurant. That night we slept on board in the harbor of Mykonos, an island near Delos.

On deck the next morning, I found Susan having her coffee. The sea was rough. The sky above the horizon looked like steam hovering over a vat of boiling ink. I asked Susan if we were going to go straight on into this yawning hell, adding that I was not Captain Ahab. She assured me we would turn back if necessary. I staggered below for breakfast. Except for Taki and the crew, the others were asleep.

I found Taki sitting in a tiny deck house with one side open facing aft, and decided it was a good place to hole up. The sun shining through the flying spume of the sea became a cascade of glittering light. The waves sweeping around us were enormous. This I said to myself is the wine-dark sea on which Odysseus sailed. Taki smiled peacefully. The captain standing at the wheel smiled peacefully. I consigned them and Odysseus to hell.

Loomis and Jane came lurching and staggering along the deck. We shouted across the wind. They found a tarpaulin and snuggled down under it with their heads sticking out, looking like figures on an Etruscan tomb. Taki jumped up. He was just in time. Carlton and Cecelia, bent down against the wind, had almost gone overboard. Cecelia gave one baleful glare at the howling elements, and made a quick decision—back to the bunk with dramamine.

I held onto the iron rail alongside the deck house. In the wind and sun my hands felt very raw, but there was nothing I could do about it. Hours went by. I stood up and looked forward. We were poised on the crest of a wave. The boat shuddered, crashed down into the swirling trough, and banged up into the blue foaming mass ahead. I sat down. Susan struggled into the deck house. "The captain wants to know if you are afraid," she yelled in my ear. "No," I yelled

22

(Opposite Page) Mr. John Papadimitriou, Susan Saridis, and T. H. Robsjohn-Gibbings in the ruins of the fifth century B.C. Sanctuary of Artemis at Vraona near Athens. The re-created Greek klini (couch) in the foreground is placed where a couch once stood. Since this photograph was taken, Mr. Papadimitriou has supervised extensive restorations on the site. Photograph by Loomis Dean for *Life*.

24 The *Iris* sails for Delos. Photograph by Loomis Dean for *Life*.

back, "I'm just damned uncomfortable." It was true. The legend of Greek seamanship is a potent one. I was clinging to it. It was all I had to cling to.

Loomis came half out of his tarpaulin and took photographs. Jane, with her hair hanging in black wet coils, looked like Medusa. Susan and the captain shouted together in Greek. I bellowed at Susan, "Now what?" She smiled, pulled my head toward her, and shouted, "There's an island ahead. We're going there." I decided not to think about anything. The light was fading. I dozed. When I woke, the boat was not banging about any more. There were cliffs outside the porthole. I stood up. There was the stone quay, and the restaurant. We were back at Kea.

It seemed incredible that land could be walked on, incredible that it didn't move, that chairs and tables placed on it stood still. How good those cocktails were. I looked around at the sleepy cats and the geraniums growing in the whitewashed gasoline cans. Between the vine leaves growing over the arbor the stars looked like glistening blossoms. Far away up the village street someone was playing a bouzouki.

Later when Susan, Jane, and Loomis said goodnight, Cecelia, fresh from her dramamine blackout, suggested that we investigate the bouzouki music with Carlton. We found it coming from a small shop along the quay and went in. It looked like a general store. There were three tables, and some fishermen were sitting around one of them. Behind the counter was the owner, a middle-aged woman, with her handsome son. On a small platform were two bouzouki players. We sat down and ordered beer.

Two of the young men got up and danced. They had clumsy bodies, enormous feet, and were completely unself-conscious. To them we were invisible. They were repeating some ancient ritual, some almost forgotten expression of joy from the ancient past of the Cyclades. Though their olive-black eyes were expressionless, their gestures sometimes had a sly hint of male and female courtship, their movements a languorous air befitting dancers in a harem. When the music stopped, no one applauded. The dancers returned to their table. Cecelia was satisfied and we said good night. Outside the wind had vanished. The *Iris*, motionless on the still water, seemed to be asleep.

The plaintive squawk of a gull woke me. The *Iris* was moving along with a gentle rolling motion. On deck I found Susan and Taki peering under the tarpaulin that covered the furniture. A table was badly damaged. It might have been worse. We drank our coffee and sailed through a sea of wavering light between dim blue islands seemingly suspended in air. Beyond the faint line of the horizon was Piraeus.

Hours later, as we drove away from the port, I looked back. The *Iris* had disappeared in a forest of swaying masts. With the exhibition only a week away, Susan was worried. There were press releases, press luncheons, interviews, show-

25

26   (Above and Opposite Page) Views of the original exhibition of Greek furniture at Saridis of Athens. The plants are species that grew on the Acropolis in the fourth century B.C. according to ancient writers. The olive tree was sacred to Athena. Photographs by Stratis Anapliotis.

rooms to be rearranged, and a damaged table that might have to be remade. I pointed to the Parthenon standing guard in the sky. "Athena," I said, "has a big stake in it all. Don't worry."

Eleftherios had sent an invitation to Miss Gisela M. A. Richter, the foremost authority on ancient furniture, who was in Rome. She had accepted it, and two days after our return from Delos I met her and gave her a preview of the

exhibition. Gentle, serene, she examined every detail with the moving and endearing curiosity, concentration, and humility of a great scholar.

The table re-created from a limestone statuette from Cyprus (page 96) worried her. The stretcher might be incorrectly placed. She took out a tiny notebook and made a reminder to look at the original model in the British Museum. She was correct. The stretcher was changed after the exhibition. The one shown in this book is the corrected model.

It was Wednesday, May 31, 1961, the day of the opening. We hurried to the exhibition room. I had forgotten how much the Greeks love flowers. Everywhere we looked were huge bouquets, and in the entrance hall more were being delivered. The center of the long buffet was a mass of scarlet roses. In every corner were sweet peas, lilacs, cornflowers, every flower of spring. Each man from the Saridises' factory was wearing a new uniform, and Eleftherios was like a general about to go on parade.

The last flower in place, the last particle of dust removed, Susan suggested that we join the guests waiting in the entrance hall. How calm everyone was. Jane was there looking like a goddess. Then Susan and Eleftherios took their positions on the steps of the entrance. All eyes were on the center of the hall where Mr. Dimitri Levidis, Grand Marshal of the Court, was standing silhouetted against the light. Far away was a sound of clapping. It came closer. We heard the crunch of the royal tires on the gravel.

That night from our balcony, we saw the Parthenon illuminated like a vision in the sky, and we relived the day. There were recollections of gracious informality, expressions of profound understanding, warm congratulations. There was the face of a teenage carpenter looking about in awe and smiling with pleasure when a hand was put on his shoulder. There was Eleftherios overcome at the announcement that he would be awarded the Order of the Phoenix. Then there were the handshakes, curtsies, bows, goodbyes, a sense of a great occasion being ended.

That night Miss Richter flew to Rome. The following morning Loomis and Jane flew to Paris. Cecelia left for Asia Minor. Two days later Carlton and I were on our way back to America.

Greek furniture continued its journey through time.

T. H. Robsjohn-Gibbings
Athens 1961
New York 1963

Unloading Greek furniture from the *Iris*, at the quay, Delos. Photograph by Loomis Dean for *Life*.

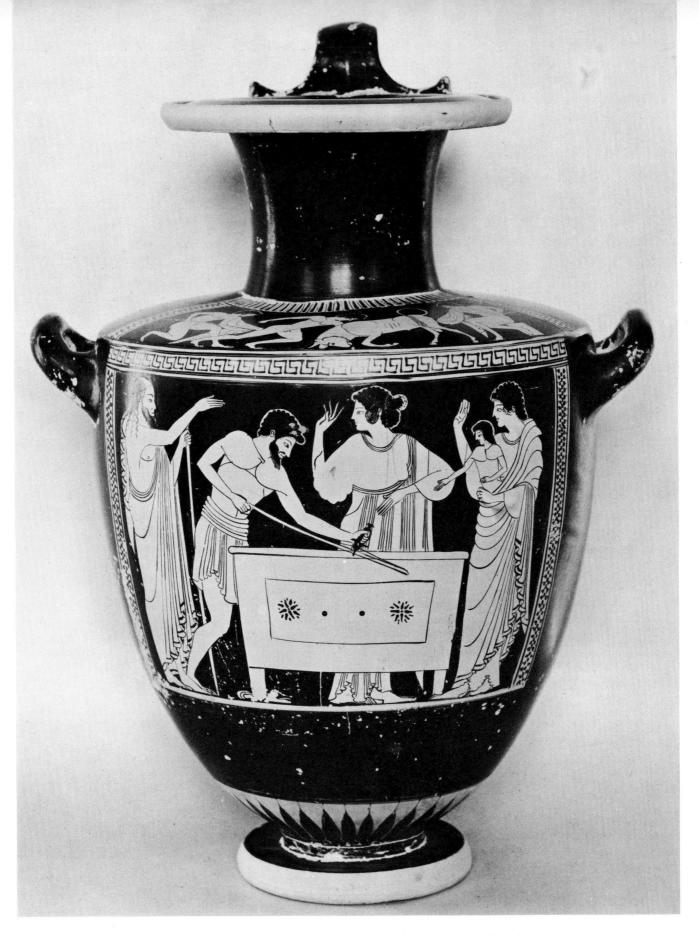

In the foreground of the scene on this Attic red-figured hydria (water jug) illustrating the legend of Danäe and Perseus is a typical Greek chest of the classical period, painted or inlaid with stellate motifs. At the left of the chest, a Greek carpenter bends forward to complete his work. Photograph courtesy of the Museum of Fine Arts, Boston.

FURNITURE OF CLASSICAL GREECE

The craftsman, looking toward the true form, so fashions.

PLATO

About 2,000 B.C. furniture of Western Asia and Egypt came to Greece via Crete and the Cyclades. During the centuries, as it crossed the Aegean, this furniture was transformed. Chairs carved on statuettes found on the Cycladic Islands and sarcophagi from the island of Crete are no longer Asian or Egyptian but the prototype of a new furniture—Greek furniture, the furniture of modern Western man.

The first shadowy forms of this Greek furniture, partly legendary, partly real, multicolored, gleaming with golden inlay, illuminated with poetic imagination, are described by Homer. About the ninth century B.C., crudely delineated in silhouettes on geometric style vases, furniture forms that are truly Greek become visible. Basically the same as a stool shown on a vase of this period is one carved in replica four hundred years later by Phidias and his sculptors on the frieze of the Parthenon.

From about the sixth century B.C., in marble reliefs, bronzes, terracotta statuettes, and painted pottery, Greek furniture stands revealed. There are seven basic models—throne-like chairs, stools, couches, footstools, tables, chests, and a

31

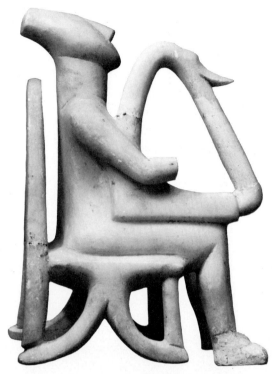

Cycladic marble statuette of a lyre player. From Keros, *circa* 2,000 B.C. In the National Archaeological Museum, Athens.

unique chair called a klismos. For at least four hundred years, from the sixth to the third centuries B.C., Greek craftsmen concentrated their imaginations and skills on these seven basic models and brought them to perfection.

In this long development, Asian and Egyptian influences, lingering in chests, couches, and throne-like chairs, were eliminated and replaced by new Greek forms. Meanwhile, Greek craftsmen invented the klismos. Perhaps the most beautiful chair extant, it has no Eastern prototype, and is truly Greek Graceful, harmonious, rising from the ground in slow sweeping curves culminating in a deep elliptical back rest, this extraordinary chair has the power to endow the sitter with nobility.

The seats of chairs, stools, and couches have leather or fiber thongs stretched across them within the frame or over it. An embroidered linen or wool mattress covers the thongs of a couch. On chairs and stools an embroidered cloth or a deer or other animal skin is sometimes placed under an embroidered cushion. Chests made of wood are polychromed in bright colors or embellished with metal or terracotta bas reliefs showing legendary figures and animals. Furniture of maple, olive, boxwood, cedar, and oak with inlays of precious metals and ivory and the use of a wax finish are mentioned by ancient Greek authors. On an oil flask of the fifth century B.C., the color of a klismos is shown. The wood is a medium to dark brown shade with darker brown leather thongs.

In the carved and painted details and embellishments of Greek furniture, from the archaic models to the perfected ones of the classical period, there is a

32

A sculptor in his studio sits on a low stool. From a bowl of the sixth century B.C. in the National Museum, Copenhagen.

suggestion of the environment and associations of Greek craftsmen. Depicted in wood carvings and in bronze are pet fawns of childhood, horned rams guarded by young shepherds, swans, deer and lions from the hunt, and acanthus, honeysuckle, laurel, and lotus flowers of spring. Doric and Ionic columns carved on the façade of a wooden chest-sarcophagus and the arm posts of a chair recall

33

A chorus of satyrs comes dancing on stage carrying separate parts of a couch which they assemble while keeping time to a flute. From an Attic red-figured hydria, *circa* 475-450 B.C. Photograph courtesy of the Museum of Fine Arts, Boston.

familiar temple precincts and the watching eyes of wise Athena, patron deity of Greek carpenters. In the unity of the seat-frame and the turned legs of stools and couches are the designers' observations of trees and their organic fusion of trunk and branch. In the stellate motifs of a chest are their memories of night skies and a flight of stars.

On chairs and stools, carved and inlaid with ivory and gold, are familiar supernal beings: Pegasus drops from the sky on voluted wings, griffins and harpies crouch ready to vanish into space, majestic Nereids mounted on plunging sea horses and sea serpents ride the Aegean's waves. Knowing that the gods regarded their furniture with envy, Greek craftsmen made it worthy of them. Zeus, Athena, Poseidon, Dionysus, and other Olympians are depicted on stools and klismoi that undoubtedly duplicate those used by mortals.

Greek passion for perfection and Greek faith in traditional forms, concentrated for centuries on this furniture, gave it the authority and power to transcend time. In its highest development, the furniture suggests the lean, sinewy

34

A girl brings a small chest to an older woman. From an Attic white-ground lekythos (oil jug), *circa* 440 B.C. Photograph courtesy of the Museum of Fine Arts, Boston.

A boy, bending under the weight, carries a couch and table on his bare back in preparation for a banquet. A drawing from a pelike (amphora) of the second quarter of the fifth century B.C. in the Ashmolean Museum, Oxford, England.

modeling of an athlete, the grace of a wild animal in repose. Where constructional strength is increased at the intersection of vertical and horizontal members, the form assumes the frank beauty of a muscle in a shoulder or a thigh. Leather strapping instead of upholstery leaves the form bare. Never again would furniture be so joyous, so virile, so lucid. Never again would furniture forms reflect such total responsiveness to life.

In almost every representation of Greek life the furniture is present. In scenes on painted vases and on carvings this Greek world is visible. A teacher in the schoolroom with a boy learning to play the lyre sit gravely face to face on leather-thonged stools. A physician seated on a folding stool examines a sick boy. A young naked bronze worker filing a helmet in his workshop and a sculptor in his studio sit on low stools. A painter of pottery sits on a klismos with his implements on a low three-legged table beside him. In a shoemaker's shop a customer stands on a bronze-legged table while she is being fitted by the owner seated on a stool. In the palaestra, two athletes seated on stools urge a leashed cat and dog to fight. A youth about to rub his body with oil lays his mantle on a folding stool. Two bearded warriors wearing helmets and greaves, their shields beside them, sit on square stools opposite a low table on which they are playing a game with dice. White-bearded and corpulent, two old councilors sitting on klismoi bend forward to whisper diplomatic secrets.

Crowded together in the steep sunlit tiers of a theater, Greek audiences saw familiar furniture on the stage. In the grotesque pageantry of a satyr play, Dionysus and Ariadne recline on a couch and a flute player sits on a klismos encircled by cavorting satyrs. In a scene from an Attic comedy, a chorus of satyrs come dancing on stage carrying separate parts of a couch, which they assemble while keeping time to a flute. In a tragi-comedy, a slave dashes to the wings with a circular bronze-legged table and a comic actor dressed as a mincing, dancing mistress sits on a klismos and rattles enormous castanets.

In the privacy of their homes, the Greeks used this same basic furniture—with additional models necessary for a domestic life. Greek houses of the fifth to fourth century B.C. found at Olynthus are built with adobe brick, two stories high around a sunlit central court, and are spacious, well-lighted, temperate, and soundproof. In the main areas, walls banded in white and vermilion frame floors of pebble mosaic. Tile bathrooms with drainage systems are equipped with terracotta tubs, wash basins, and latrines.

Interior scenes of such houses painted on Greek pottery, carved in marble reliefs and in bronze and terracotta statuettes, portray Greek families at home with their furniture. Hanging on the walls of the house, in the same way that manual instruments for fashioning leather or bronze hung on the walls of Greek shops and foundries, are implements of life—cups, lyres, castanets, flutes, writing tablets, work baskets, hand mirrors, wine jugs, oil flasks, sandals, helmets, swords, and shields.

At a late banquet, male carousers caressed by jeweled hetairae recline on couches. In front of the couches are bronze-legged tables. On the right, a small slave boy serving wine holds a jug and a strainer. A drawing from an Athenian red-figured kylix (drinking cup), *circa* 490-480 B.C., in the Metropolitan Museum of Art, New York City.

In the seclusion of a bedroom in the women's quarters, a slim naked girl, with a vase of perfume at her feet, reaches for a tunic on a klismos. Another girl already dressed, seated on a stool, bends forward and ties a thonged sandal. A woman on a klismos holds up a mirror and arranges her hair, and a maid brings a jewel case to her mistress seated on a stool. Gathered around a deer-legged table, two young girls seated on a klismos and a stool, a caged bird at their side, make cakes. In the kitchen quarters, serving women crouched on low stools, grate cheese, stir a casserole, and guard the oven fire under the baking bread.

Filling the house with fragrance, clothes and sandals are perfumed for a feast. A girl takes the clothes from a klismos and places them on a stool suspended over hot embers on which her companion pours perfume. In another room, a girl puts away clothes piled on a stool. Elsewhere a woman opens the lid of a chest to store folded linen. Chattering women seated on klismoi, preparing material for weaving clothes, roll unspun wool on a bare leg and spin with distaff and spindle.

In other areas of the house, perhaps the interior court, a baby's bed is wheeled into the sun, naked children feed a pet raven perched on a stool, climb a bronze-legged table, and reach up to their mother seated on a klismos. There are sounds of music in the house. A young girl seated on a stool practices on a flute; a woman seated on a klismos sings to the accompaniment of a lyre. Somewhere in the recesses of the women's quarters, perhaps in the drowsy quiet of a midday siesta, an old woman sleeps on a low bed, her bare breasts pressed against the leather thongs.

Other scenes show furniture in use in the masculine areas of the house. A warrior son, Neoptolemos, his sword belted across his bared body, his friend by his side, says goodbye to his father who is seated on a klismos. A boy, bending under the weight, carries a couch and table on his bare back in preparation for a banquet. In the late afternoon, the men of the house, bathed, relaxing on couches with embroidered pillows and cushions, their wives sometimes on chairs beside them, are served a meal on low tables of bronze and wood. At late banquets, reclining on similar couches, male carousers, wreathed, caressed by jeweled hetairae, pour libations, watch a chosen boy dance to the music of a flute and throw the wine lees from their drinking cups in a game of kottabos.

In more intimate scenes a young man relaxed on a klismos anticipates the embraces of a naked girl. Later, leaving fellow revelers snoring against bronze table legs, one, unclothed, finds his way through the summer night and knocks with the butt end of a torch on a bronze studded door. Behind it holding a lighted lamp is his wife.

Beautiful, practical, impervious to time, the furniture outlived this bright Greek world that nurtured it. The Greeks themselves, conquering, colonizing, and trading, planted their furniture designs over distances touching the Black

38

Sea, Asia Minor, Upper Egypt, North Africa, the Pillars of Hercules, Spain, France, and Italy. In sites as far apart as Luxor, Egypt, and Panticapaeum and the Crimea in Russia, archaeologists have found crumbling models of original Greek furniture.

When Greece faltered and Rome took command in the second century B.C., Greek furniture began its long journey through time. Roman matrons and dignitaries recline on ponderous klismoi and sleep on bulbous-legged couches veneered with bone and inlaid with tinted glass. Byzantine rulers sit erect on rigid Greco-Roman thrones and benches now overlaid with beaten gold and jeweled encrustations symbolic of Heavenly wealth. Greek chests, folding benches, throne-like chairs and circular three-legged tables, surviving in almost their original form, appear in Gothic interiors of the thirteenth century A.D.

The classical revival of the Renaissance, using debased Roman versions of Greek furniture, produced coffers with lion's feet, folding stools, high-back chairs terminating in lion's claws, and doors studded in bronze. In seventeenth and eighteenth century France and England, folding stools, arm chairs, and particularly daybeds were—for all the additions of carved rococo ornamentation—derived from the Greeks. On its odyssey through time and space, Greek furniture came even to America. Seventeenth century American chairs, known as Pilgrim chairs, with turned arm and back posts and slat backs; seventeenth century chests; and daybeds of the seventeenth and early eighteenth centuries had their ancestry in Greek designs.

In the romantic climate of the eighteenth century, awareness of antiquity was stirring again. Eighteenth century imaginations, brooding in the eerie ruins of Piranesi, scanning the manuscript drawings of Palladio, and dreaming in the golden landscapes of Panini, were spellbound by the mystery and allure of pagan life. The stage was set for the Greek Revival.

Unlike the Renaissance, which was limited to Roman versions of Greek design, the Greek Revival sprang from the rediscovery of ancient Greece itself. In the middle of the eighteenth century, Greece and Greek architecture, so far away in time, so lost, so inaccessible, became suddenly visible again, measured, engraved, and bound in sumptuous folios. Fired by dreams of classical antiquity, English lords in lumbering coaches trailed by galloping retinues of valets, chefs, and architects, headed for Italy and Greece to study, document, and loot the defenseless past. In London, Paris, Munich, and St. Petersburg, the rococo dead in its wake, the Greek Revival swept into power. Traveling in France, Horace Walpole stared. "Everything," he pouted, "must be *à la grecque.*"

And it was. In England, Sheraton attempted "Grecian sofas." In France, Percier and Fontaine, creating an *ambiance* of deification for Napoleon I, scattered Greek motifs over Empire furniture. In 1807 the English architect Thomas Hope, who had studied in Greece, published *Household Furniture and Decora-*

39

tion. A flood of Regency klismoi, *neo Grec* sofas, tables, and stools, together with ladies in high-waisted, neo-hetairae dresses swept over England.

Despite the ardor of its first promoters, Greek Revival furniture could not transcend the elaboration demanded by and identified with rich Europeans who purchased it. Information and scholarly research on Greek furniture were lacking. As a result Greek architectural motifs unrelated to Greek furniture were imposed on eighteenth century furniture forms, and Greek furniture was misinterpreted and given eighteenth century embellishments.

A woman seated on a klismos and two standing women feed cranes. From a red-figured hydria of the fifth century B.C. Photograph courtesy of the Fogg Art Museum, Harvard University, Cambridge, Massachusetts.

40

For no eighteenth or nineteenth century furniture designer realized that Greek furniture had a spirit, form, and proportion that belonged to it and to it alone. In the neo-Greek salons of Robert Adam, the Empire boudoirs of Empress Josephine and Madame Récamier was furniture with hazy reference to Greece but no Greek furniture.

By the end of the first half of the nineteenth century, this taste for Grecian furniture, debased and made commonplace in the Greco-bourgeois parlors of Herr Biedermeier, began to sink into oblivion. But there were dying echoes. Chairs and sofas "in the Greek Taste" wander through Victorian Europe and emigrate to America under the auspices of Duncan Phyfe. Inspired by the "Grecian Courts" of the Great Exhibition of 1851, cast iron "Grecian" furniture moved into humid Victorian conservatories. But finally, a minor driftage in the rising tide of Edwardian eclecticism, furniture with reference to Greece vanished.

But now almost two hundred years after Greek Revival days, archaeologists with spades, trowels, aerial photography, sounding and draining equipment, and electronic cameras, have moved away the earth between us and the Greek past. Temples, once tumbled ruins, stand erect in the sun. Greek cities and sites, once mounds known only to goatherds and their flocks, reappear and reveal the ancient past. We stroll again in colonnaded streets, sit on marble seats in a theater, linger in a palaestra, and rest in the shade of a stoa. We cross the thresholds of Greek houses, walk on mosaic floors, touch the waxed surfaces of frescoed walls, and examine terracotta hip baths, wash basins, and water pipes running underground to mountains sometimes ten miles away.

We see in actuality cosmetic jars, mirrors, tweezers, hairpins, and jewelry used and worn by Greek women. We see the vessel in which the wine was mixed with water, the ladle for serving the wine and the cups from which it was drunk. We see the pots and pans used in a Greek kitchen.

In museums scattered across Europe we see in reality some Greek furniture. There are broken remains of tables in Brussels, Paris, Palermo, and London. There are chests in Russia and Germany.

But knowledge of Greek furniture is not limited to these precious fragments. Carved in marble, cast in bronze and terracotta, and painted in scenes on over one hundred thousand Greek vases, the furniture of Greece, drawn by Greek artists, stands before us, irrefutable, noble, timeless.

KLISMOI

Klismos (foreground) on an earthen plaque of the middle of the sixth century B.C. Photograph copyright the State Museum, Berlin.

CHAIR (Klismos)
Walnut chair with leather thongs on seat, a re-creation of the Greek chair shown at left. One of the earliest models shown in this book, this klismos has not assumed the sweeping curves and elliptical back rest that were developed later. The severe grace and bold contours of this chair recall a similar severity and grace seen in archaic Greek sculpture.

CHAIR (Klismos)
The klismos, the most beautiful of all Greek furniture designs, was developed and perfected over a long period of time. The chair shown here, re-created from a drawing on an oil jug of the fifth century B.C., is the klismos in its perfected form. A masterpiece of Greek art, it has no prototype in Egypt or western Asia. It is a Greek invention. On Greek vases, the klismos often appears in use in the women's quarters of a Greek house, but occasionally it is depicted in use on the Greek stage and in other public places. The color of the walnut of this klismos closely approximates that of a klismos shown on a white-ground oil jug of the fifth century B.C. (see page facing 94). The medium-dark tone of the wood emphasizes the bold silhouette of the chair. The darker tone of the leather thongs adds richness but does not distract from the harmonious, flowing lines of the form. Photograph, William Maris, Stoller Associates.

Klismos painted on a vase of the first quarter of the fifth century B.C.
Photograph copyright the State Museum, Berlin.

CHAIR (Klismos)
Walnut chair with leather thongs on seat, a re-creation of the Greek chair shown at left. The austere beauty of this klismos is an interesting contrast to the sweeping crescent shapes of later chairs. The fielded panels on the legs are an interesting detail that occurs frequently on chairs of this period.

Woman placing an embroidered seat cushion on a klismos. In this instance a diaphanous cover sewn with flower-like motifs bordered with a wave pattern has already been placed over the seat. From a fifth century B.C. wine vessel. Photograph courtesy of the Hermitage, Leningrad.

Satyr carrying a klismos. The drawing clearly shows the leather thongs on the seat. From a fifth century B.C. krater (wine-mixing vessel). Photograph courtesy of the British Museum, London.

Chair with a loose, embroidered seat cushion. From a red-figured Athenian lekythos, *circa* 430-420 B.C. Photograph courtesy of the Metropolitan Museum of Art, Fletcher Fund, 1930, New York City.

Klismos painted on a lekythos of the fifth century B.C.
Photograph courtesy of Ashmolean Museum, Oxford, England.

CHAIR (Klismos)
Walnut chair with leather thongs on seat, a re-creation of the Greek chair shown at left. On the original drawing from which this design was taken, a raised, tapering panel is indicated on the sides of the legs. This detail does not show very clearly in the photograph of the vase. But it is a very important part of the design of this particular klismos, one of the most beautiful in the repertoire of Greek chairs. The legs, sweeping upward from the floor, increasing in strength where they are intersected by the seat frame, have a lithe, muscular quality.

Small klismos (at left) painted on a red-figured Athenian lebes gamikos (wedding basin), *circa* 430-420 B.C., in the Metropolitan Museum of Art, New York City.

CHAIR (Klismos)
Walnut chair with leather thongs on seat, a re-creation of the Greek chair shown at left. The back rest of this klismos is lower than that of the typical Greek klismos of the period, and the legs are less curved and are lighter in scale. The smaller proportions of this klismos are evident when compared with a chair of the usual dimensions shown in the same drawing. The diminuation of the chair does not involve any loss of character. It is a confident, spirited design with the verve and vitality typical of Greek furniture.

CHAIR (Klismos)

Walnut chair with leather thongs on seat, a re-creation of the Greek chair shown at right. The model of the chair carved on this famous stele is one of the most valuable pieces of evidence on the proportions and design of a klismos. Shown with accuracy and detail, this sculptured chair is only slightly smaller in size than an actual Greek klismos. The Greek sculptor has copied with great fidelity an actual chair, showing accurately the proportions of the members, the sweep of the leg, the height of the seat, and the form of the back post and back rest. Only the width of the chair and the center panel of the back are not shown. In re-creating this chair and filling in the lacunae, information was obtained from a three-dimensional bronze miniature in the British Museum, drawings on vases, and Greek theater seats carved in marble in the design of a klismos.

Klismos on the stele of Hegeso, *circa* 400 B.C., in the National Archaeological Museum, Athens.

DIPHROI

Folding stool (behind chair) on an earthen plaque of the middle of the sixth century B.C. Photograph copyright the State Museum, Berlin.

FOLDING STOOL (Diphros Okladias)
Walnut folding stool with leather top and bronze ferrules, crossbar, and pivotal pins, a re-creation
of the Greek folding stool shown in elevation on the earthen plaque at left. Stools of this type have
Egyptian origins, but the sweeping lines of the leg carved in the design of the leg and hoof of a deer
are characteristically Greek. Light and portable, folding stools are often shown in outdoor scenes as
well as in household scenes on Greek vases.

Folding stool on a Greek bronze mirror stand of the fifth century B.C. Photograph courtesy of the Museum of Fine Arts, Boston.

71

Stool painted on a kyathos (wine-ladling cup), *circa* 490-480 B.C. Photograph courtesy of the State Museum, East Berlin.

STOOL (Diphros)
Four-legged walnut stool with leather thongs outside the frame, a re-creation of the Greek stool shown at left. Throughout the repertoire of Greek stools, although the basic form remains constant, Greek craftsmen invented innumerable sculptural details at the intersection of the leg and seat rail. In this instance, the seat rail and leg are joined with a spherical form, and there is a noticeable absence of architectural derivation. Though the basic elements of the stool are simplified, a rich sculptural effect is achieved.

74

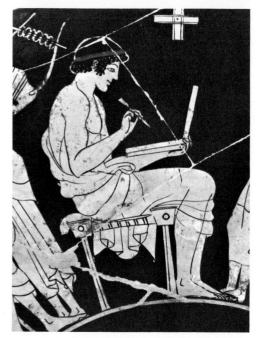

Stool painted on a kylix, *circa* 480 B.C. Photograph copyright the State Museum, Berlin.

STOOL (Diphros)
Four-legged walnut stool with leather thongs outside the frame, a re-creation of the Greek stool shown at left. Stools of this type were very popular in classical Greece. Drawings on Greek vases show the stool in use in the house, schoolroom, workshop, and palaestra. The fine proportions and sturdy grace of this stool made it the prototype of similar European stools over the following two thousand years.

Stool painted on a kylix, *circa* 480 B.C., in a private collection in England. Photograph, D. Widmer, Basel.

STOOL (Diphros)

Four-legged walnut stool with leather thongs outside the frame, a re-creation of the Greek stool shown at left. The drawing of the stool on the vase shows leather thongs arranged in groups of four. The design of the leg is a bold, elongated, tapering block under which the form narrows and flares gently downward to its base. The dowel on the leg, an important part of the design, follows exactly the outline of the block. In contrast to the rounded contours of the stool selected by Phidias for the Parthenon frieze (see page 84), this stool is uncompromisingly angular; but its bold, forceful silhouette makes a noble base for a seated figure.

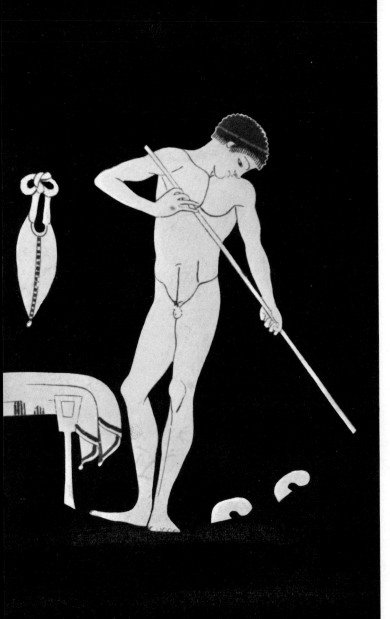

Stool painted on a kylix, *circa* 470 B.C. Photograph copyright
the State Museum, Berlin.

82

STOOL (Diphros)

Four-legged walnut stool with leather thongs outside the frame, a re-creation of the Greek stool shown at left. Stools with curving legs are rare in Greek furniture. This stool has legs with a graceful, pronounced concave silhouette. The design of the upper part of the leg is a bold, tapering block with the corner edge continuing downward in an unbroken curve to the base. The combination of rhythmic strength, grace, and symmetry of this stool make it comparable to the finest Greek sculpture of the period.

83

Stools carved on the Parthenon frieze, *circa* 442-438 B.C., in the Acropolis Museum, Athens.

STOOL (Diphros)
Four-legged walnut stool with leather thongs inside the frame, a re-creation of the Greek stool carved by Phidias and his sculptors on the frieze shown at left. Comparison with stools of this design shown on Greek vases of the ninth to eighth centuries B.C. indicates that Greek craftsmen spent over four hundred years perfecting the stool before achieving the beauty of this model made in the fifth century B.C. Where strength is necessary at the top of the leg, the form —bold and rounded—merges with the horizontal seat frame in one unbroken surface. The stool has the intrinsic confidence, serenity, and nobility identified with the finest achievements of Greek architecture.

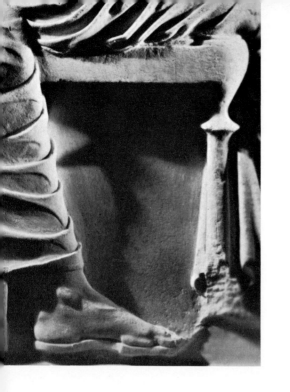

Miniature terracotta Greek stool of the fifth century B.C. Photograph courtesy of the Museum für antike Kleinkunst, Munich.

STOOL (Diphros)

Four-legged walnut stool with leather thongs inside the frame, a re-creation of the Greek stool shown at left. The terracotta miniature model is of special interest, for in the recessed area on its top, painted lines indicate fiber or leather thongs set inside the frame. The proportions of the miniature show that this type of classical Greek stool was square. In re-creating the stool, crudely modeled in the miniature, some refinements have been made. Without any sculptural forms other than the modified finial at the top of the leg, the stool, with its fastidious proportions and characteristic blending of seat rail and leg, is timeless.

STOOL (Diphros)

Four-legged walnut stool with leather thongs inside the frame, a re-creation of the Greek stool shown at right in elevation. This stool has the beautiful, characteristically Greek construction in which the face of the horizontal seat frame merges with the rounded form of the leg. The dignity and nobility of the seated figure on the stele is enhanced by the intrinsic nobility of the stool.

Stool carved on the stele of Eupraxis and Miltiades, fifth to fourth century B.C., in the National Archaeological Museum, Athens.

93

This painting on an Attic white-ground oil jug in the Museum of Fine Arts, Boston, shows a klismos in color. The wood is a medium to dark brown tone. The thongs, probably of leather, are slightly darker. The drawing on this vase was used as a guide for the color of the walnut and leather of the re-created models of Greek furniture shown in this book. Photograph by Edward Moore. Courtesy of the Museum.

TRAPEZAI

Table on a limestone statuette from Cyprus of the sixth century B.C. in the British Museum, London.

TABLE (Trapeza)
Three-legged walnut table, a re-creation of the Greek table shown
at left. The design of the leg is like that of an architectural pilaster. The
rounded molding at its edge enclosing a convex panel is unique. The
rectangular form of the top is shown very clearly on the statuette, and
stretchers are indicated. Some refinements of details have been made
on the re-created model.

99

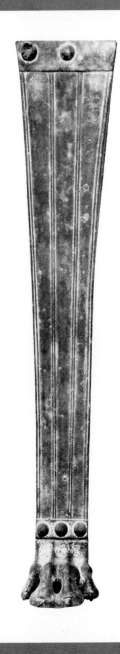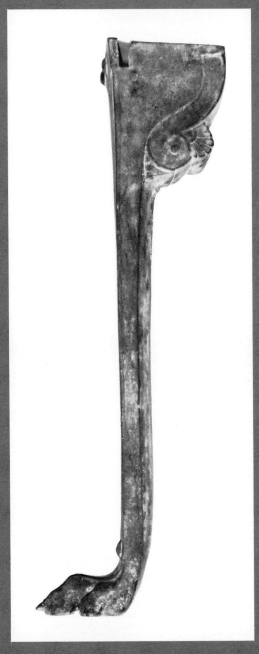

Original bronze table leg. Photograph courtesy of the Palermo Museum, Sicily.

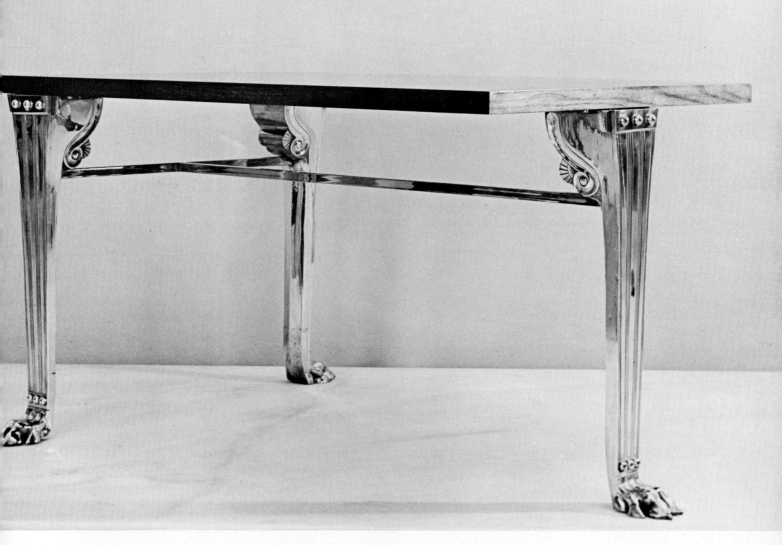

TABLE (Trapeza)
Table with walnut top and three bronze legs and stretchers, a re-creation of the Greek table
shown on a kylix, at top of page 103. The legs of this table, executed in the design of a
reeded pilaster terminating in a lion's paw, were cast in bronze from an original leg in the
Palermo Museum, shown at left. On vases, tables of this type are frequently depicted
alongside couches for dining. One advantage of a three-legged table is its stability on an
uneven floor. This table is one of the masterpieces of Greek art.

Youth dancing on a table. This bronze statuette shows clearly the form of the table and the placement of the three legs. From the State Museum, Berlin.

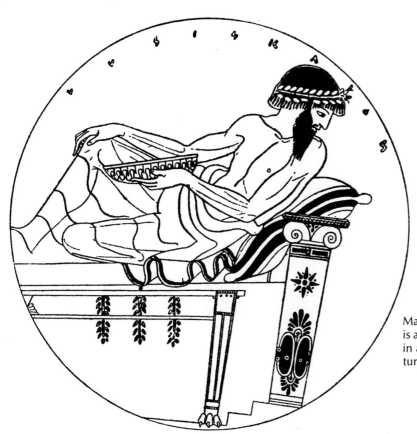

Man reclining on a couch. Beside the couch is a table clearly showing the leg terminating in a lion's paw. From a kylix of the fifth century B.C. in the State Museum, Berlin.

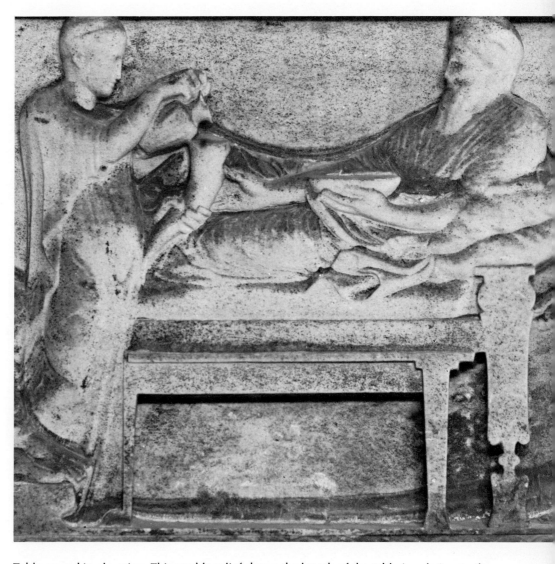

Table carved in elevation. This marble relief shows the length of the table in relation to the height of the leg. From a carved marble panel of the fifth century B.C. in the Archaeological Museum, Istanbul.

TABLE (Trapeza)
Three-legged walnut table, a re-creation of the Greek table shown at right. This table has the lightness and grace characteristic of Greek design. The form and curving silhouette of the legs recall the beauty of a klismos. The sides of the rectangular top, in a design of three receding planes, suggest the form of an architrave in an entablature.

Table painted on an Attic hydria of the fifth
century B.C. in a private collection in Milan.

Table on a lekanis (bowl), *circa* 400
B.C. Photograph courtesy of the
Hermitage, Leningrad. Wooden leg
from Panticapaeum, Russia. Photograph copyright the British Museum, London.

TABLE (Trapeza)
Three-legged walnut table, a re-creation of the Greek table shown at left. Tables of this design became popular in Greek households of the late classical period. Banquet scenes on Apulian vases sometimes show several of these three-legged tables placed beside couches. The legs of the table are carved in the design of a deer's leg and hoof. An actual three-legged Greek wooden table of this type, found in Egypt, is now in the Brussels Museum. A wooden leg (shown at left below) of a similar table found at Panticapaeum, and now in the British Museum, was used as a guide for the form and proportion of the leg of the re-created table.

Table painted on an Apulian vase of the fifth century B.C. Photograph courtesy of the Metropolitan Museum of Art, Rogers Fund, 1914, New York City.

TABLE (Trapeza)

Three-legged walnut table, a re-creation of the Greek table shown above. This type of circular table is frequently seen in banquet scenes on Apulian vases from Italy and is often represented in miniature terracotta models. In the Hellenistic period it was evidently a popular form. Although this table is lower and smaller in scale than most Greek tables, it has the clarity and order characteristic of Greek design.

Table on the stele of Gelon and Kallistratos of the fourth century B.C. in the National Archaelogical Museum, Athens. Photography by Byron Adamtziloglou.

TABLE (Trapeza)

Four-legged walnut table, a re-creation of the Greek table shown at left. This table shows the use of architectural forms applied to furniture for domestic use. The top of the table, extended downward to form a block on the corner, and the setback of the simple, tapering leg suggest an architectural pilaster. Smaller and lighter in design than earlier tables, this model still has the forthright character and nobility of Greek design.

Circular table (left) painted on a Campanian bell krater (wine-mixing vessel) of the third quarter of the fourth century B.C. Photograph courtesy of National Museum, Naples.

This vase painting shows a group of young people gathered for a party. On the left, a girl plays a flute. A man on a couch listens with rapt attention. In the center, a girl caresses her handsome companion reclining on a couch. On the right, a young man looks at a flying dove over a boy serving wine. Two tables with drinking cups and food on them stand in front of the couches. The table on the right is rectangular with three legs. The table on the left is circular with three legs identical in design with those on the rectangular table. A stretcher between the legs of the circular one is clearly indicated. From the various representations of these tables, it is evident that the same leg—presumably bronze—was used on rectangular and circular forms. In the foreground of the far right, is a bronze kottabos stand used for a game in which the wine lees in a drinking cup, held with the index finger, were thrown at a small disc balanced on the top of the kottabos stand. If the player was successful, the disc slid down the stem of the stand and struck a stationary disc below with a ringing sound.

110

TABLE (Trapeza)
Table with walnut top and three bronze legs and stretchers, a re-creation of the Greek model shown at left. The legs, in the design of a reeded pilaster terminating in a lion's paw, were cast in bronze from an original leg in the Palermo Museum, Sicily. In this photograph the console design with a volute and a palmette at the top back of the leg is clearly shown. Like the rectangular table with the same leg (see page 101), this circular table is a masterpiece of Greek art.

KLINI AND KIBOTOS

Couch painted on a red-figured kylix, *circa* 465-460 B.C., recently discovered in Spina, Italy. Photograph, Hirmer Verlag, Munich.

114

COUCH (Klini)
Walnut couch with leather thongs on seat, a re-creation of the Greek couch shown at left. Early Greek couches show Egyptian influences, but over the centuries Greek craftsmen developed this type which is completely Greek in character. The graceful, practical form of the back rest recalls the similar beauty and grace of the klismos. For dining and banquets, embroidered mattresses and luxurious cushions were used on the couch. For sleeping, bedclothes of linen or wool, often perfumed, were added.

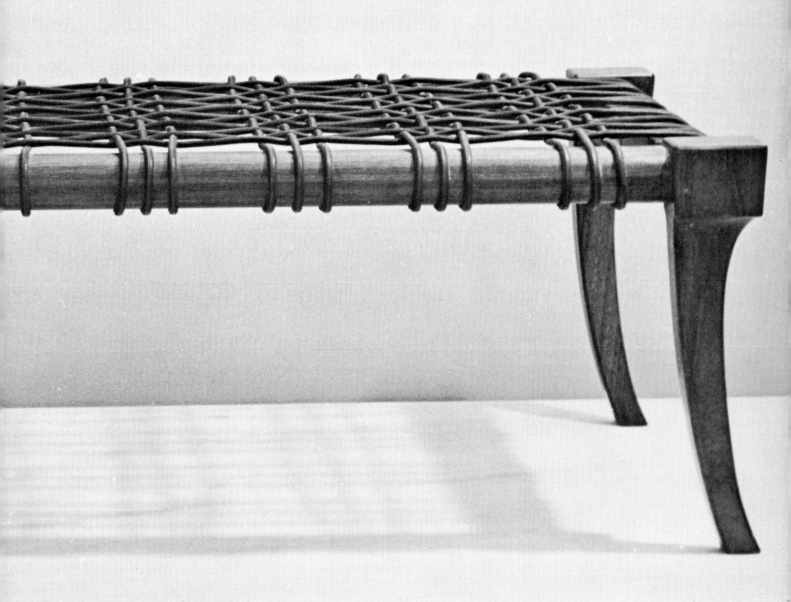

Chest on an Apulian vase of the fourth century B.C. in the Archaeological Museum, Madrid.

CHEST (Kibotos)
Chest in walnut with studs, rosettes, and Greek key design in relief and polychrome decoration, a re-creation of the Greek chest shown at left. The lucidity and precision of this chest's form recall the simplicity and strength of early Doric architecture.

CHEST (Kibotos)
The general form of Greek chests was developed in Egypt, but Greek craftsmen evolved new crea-
tions, characteristically Greek, which transcended the prototypes. The chest shown here was
re-created from a drawing on an Apulian vase of the fourth century B.C. On vase drawings and in
sculptured reliefs, chests shown in Greek interiors were used for storing clothing and household
linen. Occasionally, a seated figure shows the chest's use as a seat. Greek chests of the fourth century B.C. actually exist. These chests combine wood with polychromed designs in brilliant colors.
The colors on the re-created chest in this photograph were taken from a polychromed chest found at
Abusir and now in the museum at Hanover. Re-created chest in the collection of Mr. and Mrs.
Nicholas Goulandris.

NOTES ON THE FABRICS

NOTES ON THE FABRICS USED WITH THE GREEK FURNITURE SHOWN IN THIS BOOK

Three fabrics of classical Greece were re-created to cover pillows and a mattress shown on the furniture in this book. The pattern of a stripe painted on the kylix shown below was printed on linen in colors taken from a fragment of an altar of the sixth century B.C. A variation of this stripe painted on the kylix shown opposite (top) was also made. Another fabric, combining a pattern of plain and point-edged stripes painted on the psychter (wine cooler) shown opposite (below),

From a kylix of the fifth century B.C. in the National Museum, Copenhagen.

From a kylix of the fifth century B.C. Photograph copyright the British Museum, London.

was printed on linen in colors taken from an oil flask of the fifth century B.C. A third fabric, linen embroidered with gold thread in a diaper pattern enclosing lions, was re-created from an actual fabric of the late fifth century B.C. found at Koropi, near Volos. It is now in the Victoria and Albert Museum, London. All fabrics made by Piraiki-Patraiki, Athens.

From a psychter of the sixth century B.C. in the Hermitage, Leningrad.

NOTES ABOUT THE AUTHORS

T. H. ROBSJOHN-GIBBINGS was born in London. Originally headed for a career in architecture, he came to New York, became a citizen and an internationally known designer of interiors and furniture. He has written three best-selling books, *Good-bye, Mr. Chippendale,* a satire on antique collecting (1944); *Mona Lisa's Mustache,* a dissection of modern art (1947); and *Homes of the Brave,* an ironic look at the "modern" house (1954). His articles have appeared in *Harper's Bazaar, Town and Country, Reader's Digest, House Beautiful,* and other magazines. Between his travels to architectural sites in Egypt, Italy, and Greece, he can be found at his drawing board in New York, on the beach at Southampton, Long Island, or on the terrace of his apartment in Athens.

CARLTON W. PULLIN was born in Caesar, Texas. He was graduated *magna cum laude* from the University of Texas and worked as a magazine editor in Texas and New York. He was with the promotion department of City College of New York before turning to interior design. He has been associated with T. H. Robsjohn-Gibbings for over fifteen years and has traveled extensively in Egypt, Italy, and Greece, where much of the fieldwork was done for this book.

Bronze worker. From a kylix in the Ashmolean Museum, Oxford, England.

The joy of life is written upon everything the Greeks left behind.

EDITH HAMILTON

A NOTE ON THE TYPE

The text of this book has been set on the Linotype in a type-face called BASKERVILLE. The face is a facsimile reproduction of type cast from molds made for John Baskerville (1706-75) from his designs. The punches for the revived Linotype Baskerville were cut under the supervision of the English printer George W. Jones.

John Baskerville's original face was one of the forerunners of the type-style known as "modern face" to printers: a "modern" of the period A.D. 1800.

The captions have been set in Optima, designed by the contemporary German designer Hermann Zapf.

Composed by Haber Typographers Inc., New York
Printed by Reehl Litho. Inc., New York
Bound by H. Wolff, New York
Typography by
A. CHRISTOPHER SIMON